WHEN TRAGEDY *strikes*

7-DAY DEVOTIONAL TO OVERCOME GRIEF

Precious J. Taylor

Dedication

This book is dedicated to all who have survived losing a loved one and overcame grief. May the peace of the Lord continuously be your portion as you continue in Him for the rest of your days.

Introduction

Three shots ricocheted off my bedroom window, and I was startled by three loud screams that changed the course of my life. As those resounding shots continued to bounce off my bedroom window, I quickly recalled that my brother Derrell had been outside earlier in the day so I ran to see if he was okay. I approached the door desperately and bolted out of the house without shoes. Next, I heard a hollow voice buried in tears call out to me. Disoriented and frantic, I walked toward the voice. It cried out again, saying, "He is lying here. Derrell has been shot!" My heart dropped. My immediate reaction was to tell my mother, who was in the middle of preparing dinner for my family. I yelled, "Mom, come quickly! Derrell has been shot and he's not doing well!" My mother,always considerably calm, came out of the house quickly and asked where he was. I pointed her in the direction of the next block. She ran toward him, knelt and began to tell him that he was going to be okay.

Weakened from losing a significant amount of blood Derrell said, "Mom, I'm getting ready to die. They shot me." My mom, not accepting what Derrell was saying, continued to tell him that he would be okay.

Soon my dad, coming home from his second job, pulled up and jumped out of his Buick. Dad began to walk toward the ambulance, which had just arrived. The look on my father's face reflected deep concern, fear, and shock. The paramedics placed Derrell in the ambulance. My mother instructed me to go home with my Aunt Valda, who was now on the scene. Although I wanted to go the hospital to make sure Derrell was okay, I listened to my mother. I had been at Aunt Valda's house for nearly three hours when the phone rang. "He didn't make it!" Valda cried out. I ran to the back room, collapsed on my knees and began to cry. The words she had spoken seemed to tear the center of my soul.

The two years that followed Derrell's death were full of sleepless nights, angry outbursts, and uncertainty. In addition to feeling all of this, I also had to mentally, physically, and emotionally prepare myself to attend both the trial and the sentencing of the two defendants, who were responsible for my brother's death. Erin Grainger was the prosecutor who represented the State. Counselor Grainger was brilliant and completely dedicated to bringing justice to my family.

Counselor Grainger became the voice of my brother, as if he spoke from the grave. Her opening statement was imbued with the remnants of Derrell's life and with his legacy. Approximately a year after the trial came the sentencing for the last defendant. During this time, I had wrapped up the second semester of my undergraduate studies. My mother called and asked me to do the unthinkable: give the Victim's Impact Statement on behalf of my family. After taking a deep breath, I agreed to do it. The afternoon when the sentencing took place was unforgettable. I looked at my reflection in my bedroom window as I tried to prepare myself to be the voice of Derrell. While I was fully aware that Derrell no longer lived, a part of me felt the urge to speak as I would if he were present in the courtroom.

After arriving at the courtroom, I waited patiently for my turn to speak. I began my statement by uttering a few sentences on the impact of having lost my brother. After disclosing the impact that Derrell's death had on my family and on the entire community of those who knew and loved him, I said to the defendant, "The life that you live still contains a chance to make better decisions." The defendant looked shocked. I went on, "I extend my forgiveness to you for the choice that you have made to take the life of my brother. Now is the time for you to choose to make a meaningful change to your life.

There is still time for you to change how your story ends. After my words, the judge read his sentence. She stepped down from behind the bench and said, with her eyes full of tears, "Young lady, your words are powerful. Whatever you do in this life you will be very successful." The entire courtroom was moved. It was in that moment that I realized two important things: the power of my voice and the effect that forgiveness can have on human beings.

DAY

Now that you know my story, you can understand exactly why I am called to help those who are going through traumatic situations. October 28th, 2009, changed my life forever, everything about my brother's death was inconvenient — the fact that he died at the age of 18, just months before his high school graduation, and the fact that my parents were left to wonder what they could have done better to prevent this tragedy from occurring. All these emotions and thoughts were way too much to handle, and I found myself in a deep depression, unable to figure out what my next move should be.

Today, I would like you to consider the subject of forgiveness. Are you struggling with forgiving yourself for the death of your loved one, or struggling with forgiving your family for the death of your loved one? The most important thing to remember is that you must forgive yourself and others in order to have God forgive you. "Judge not, and you will not be judged; condemn not, and you will not be condemned; forgive, and you will be forgiven." (Luke 6:37). The principle of forgiveness is replicated from our action of forgiving ourselves and others. Whenever you are walking in condemnation and feeling inadequate, Satan, the adversary, uses it as an open door to invade your mind and heart and keep you bound by the spirit of unforgiveness.

This is the right moment for you to decide that you are done with beating yourself up for the death of your loved one and expel the spirit of unforgiveness toward yourself and family. This process of forgiveness is the first step to achieving complete healing and total deliverance from grief. By embracing the spirit of forgiveness, you are literally closing the door to Satan's ability to bring about feelings of worthlessness and self-hatred.

Today's prayer has the purpose of allowing your mind to break free from the shackles of unforgiveness, to come to a full agreement with forgiveness, and to embrace the everlasting love and forgiveness of the Father.

Father, in the name of Jesus, I come to you asking you to forgive me for having unforgiveness in my heart. Father, you say that if I don't forgive others you can't forgive me. I realize that although (insert the name of your loved one) has died, I must forgive myself and all family members who I perceive as responsible for (insert the name of your loved one)'s death. Father, I ask you to wash me clean of all unforgiveness and to give me a new perspective on life and on my situation. Father, I plead the blood of Jesus against any and all mental tormenting spirits that may try to drag me back to a negative way of thinking about myself and about others. In the name of Jesus I pray. Amen. Selah.

Now that the first day has passed, rest assured that all things are working together for your good, and that you are forgiven, loved and received by God.

Forgiveness

Write a response to today's devotion. Take a moment to reflect on what has stood out to you the most . What is God saying or speaking to you in today's devotional?

____
____
____
____
____
____
____
____
____
____
____
____
____
____

DAY

Welcome to the second day. As I grew up, my mother would always tell me that nothing but a try beats a failure. I spent years not knowing exactly what that meant. However, when I grew older I realized my mother was saying that the one and only definite way to eliminate the spirit of failure is to try again, start over with a new strategy, then take on another challenge. As you go through your healing process, you need to know that each day will indeed present a new set of obstacles, but you must be in the mindset of actively overcoming it, and be willing to allow yourself to win again. One of the biggest obstacles to people who have lost a loved one is feeling like they can't move forward. The worst enemy in the mind of the believer is the deception of thinking that their life ended when their loved one passed. I am here to tell you that this is absolutely incorrect. Our Father, God, has left you on planet Earth because there is a plan and purpose for your life, and it is entirely up to you to believe the written word of God instead of listening to the emotional enemies Satan has planted in your mind. From the word of God, we learn that Satan is the thief and he has no authority unless we give it to him.

Father, in the name of Jesus, I understand that (insert the name of your loved one) has transitioned on. You say that to be absent from the body means to be present with the Lord. I know that you left me here, on planet Earth, because there is still a plan and purpose for my life. I know that you have ordered my steps according to your word and you want me to continue to live my life in the abundance of joy, peace, and prosperity. And although (insert the name of your loved one) is gone, I know that I must go on. Lord, I ask you to help me embrace this new normal. I bind and rebuke the spirit of grief, and I prolong healing. God, according to your word in Psalms 30:5, "For his anger is but for a moment; His favor is for a life-time: Weeping may tarry for the night, But joy cometh in the morning." Lord, although my "morning" may not be right at this moment, please help me to develop an expectation that my season of joy and healing is coming. Lord, I command any foul spirit of trauma, suicide, self-harm or self-isolation to go now, in the name of Jesus. I declare and decree that I am walking into my full deliverance and freedom. In the name of Jesus I pray. Amen. Selah.

After saying this prayer, rest for ten minutes and reflect on how God, our Father, has been and will be your paragon of peace as you walk through your healing process.

Overcoming Obstacles

Write a response to today's devotion . Take a moment to reflect on what has stood out to you the most . What is God saying or speaking to you in today's devotional?

DAY

The third day has finally arrived. On this middle day, I would like to pour into your mind the strategy of the opposite. Satan, the imitator, wants to get you away from the will of God. In fact, Satan, the deceiver, is always trying to convince the believer to do and be the opposite of what God has planned for his or her life. A prime example of this was when Satan, the deceiver, tried to tempt Jesus in the wilderness. After his baptism by John the Baptist, Jesus Christ was led into the wilderness by the Holy Spirit, to be tempted by the Devil. Jesus fasted there for 40 days. Satan said, "If you are the Son of God, command this stone to become bread." (Luke 4:3, ESV). Jesus replied with Scripture, telling Satan that man does not live by bread alone. Then Satan took Jesus up and showed him all the kingdoms of the world, saying they were all under the Devil's control. He promised Jesus to give them to him if Jesus would fall down and worship the Devil. Again, Jesus quoted the Bible: "You shall worship the Lord your God, and him only shall you serve." (Deuteronomy 6:13, ESV). Satan tempted Jesus a third time by taking him to the highest point of the temple in Jerusalem and daring him to throw himself down. The Devil quoted Psalm 91:11-12, misusing the verses to imply that angels would protect Jesus. Jesus replied with Deuteronomy 6:16, ESV, "You shall not put the Lord your God to the test."

This example demonstrates how Satan comes to offer us a counterfeit of the promises of God, but we, as born again believers, must be wise and debunk Satan and his strategies with the written word of God so that we never fall for his scandalous traps. Those who are in grief are often confronted with many of Satan's lies and may end up in predicaments that in no way express the will of God for their lives. For instance, when my brother was murdered, I gained a total of 80 pounds in a little under four months and became unrecognizable to myself. This weight gain came as a result of succumbing to the enormous pressure of grief and turning to food to fill the void I felt inside, instead of turning to the word of God. Satan can and will only offer temporary fixes, whereas God offers permanent healing, this is for sure.

When we turn to God and his word for our healing, and not to people or things, we find ourselves in a much better place. Feelings and emotions correlate with your temporarily situation, not with the true reality of how things are. While you might be currently in grief, the truth is that you are sitting with Christ in heavenly places, the truth is that no weapon drawn against you shall strike, and every tongue that rises up against you in judgement shall be condemned. Repeat this prayer after me.

Father, in the name of Jesus, I come to a full agreement with your plan for my life. Although (insert the name of your loved one) is gone, I give you full permission to rule and reign in my heart. Lord, according to 2 Corinthians 10:5, I "cast down imaginations, and every high thing that exalted itself against the knowledge of God, and bringing into captivity every thought to the obedience of Christ." Lord, during my healing process, don't allow me to make emotionally irrational decisions about my life and destiny. Lord, help me to rest in your peace and safety. God, help me to run into your arms and not into the arms of people and things. Lord, I give You my thoughts and every moment of my day and ask that you regulate my mind. In the name of Jesus I pray. Amen. Selah.

Now that you have said that prayer, you can expect God, our Father, to start to manifest in your thoughts on a daily basis. Allow him to calm down your storm and get you through the troubling times ahead, on your road to healing and divine deliverance.

God Our Healer

Write a response to today's devotion . Take a moment to reflect on what has stood out to you the most . What is God saying or speaking to you in today's devotional?

____

____

____

____

____

____

____

____

____

____

____

____

____

____

____

____

DAY

Finally, you have made it to the fourth day. Having an obscured vision can cause you to make the wrong decisions. On this beautiful Thursday, I want to assist you with respect to your vision of healing. If you expect the worst, that's what will manifest and take over your life. In order to heal after having lost a loved one, it is imperative that you correct how you see yourself and the situation. When my brother passed, over eleven years ago, I remember that I thought life would never be good again for me and my family. Before being delivered, I had developed a mindset of trauma and expected the worst to happen all the time. This negative way of living is debilitating, and in no way it represents God's plan for the life of the believer. God wants you to have a fresh perspective and to expect the best, not the worst. Oftentimes, the way we see things is how things will manifest. According to Proverbs 23:7, "For as he thinketh in his heart, so is he: Eat and drink, saith he to thee; but his heart is not with thee." It is vital that you change the way you see your healing process. In order to be healed, you must allow healing to take place in you. This is done through believing that you can actually be healed, set free and delivered. Changing your vision eventually changes your thoughts, and then changes your outcome. Being completely committed to your healing is crucial, you must be dedicated enough to fight through the mercy waters of the process of healing in order to get to the other side of freedom.

Repeat this prayer : "Our Father in heaven, hallowed be your name. Your kingdom come, your will be done, on earth as it is in heaven. Give us this day our daily bread, and forgive us our debts, as we also have forgiven our debtors. And lead us not into temptation but deliver us from evil." (Matthew: 6:9-14).

Envision yourself inhaling this information through your nostrils for a moment, and allow God, our Father, to change your vision of yourself.

Write a response to today's devotion . Take a moment to reflect on what has stood out to you the most . What is God saying or speaking to you in today's devotional?

____

____

____

____

____

____

____

____

____

____

____

____

____

____

DAY

Day five and you are still alive. The road to freedom and deliverance is completely contingent on allowing God into your heart and abiding to His word. The first few months of coming to terms with my brother's death were one of the most horrific experiences I could ever imagine going through. The way I initially grieved was completely opposite to what our Father wants us to do. While it was unquestionable that I had a right to grieve, there were times when I was consumed with my emotions and didn't want a way out — I was content with feeling stuck and emotionally bound. If you are in this place, I encourage you to make a decision today that can change the rest of your life — make the decision to get unstuck by actively abiding by the word of God throughout this season.Be intentional about praying and seeking God, because the only way to see this time through is to embrace life and apply the word of God to your situation like you never did before. Jesus tells us, in Matthew 24:35, that heaven and earth shall pass away but, his words shall remain. The significance of this Scripture outweighs anything that you may experience in this lifetime. God just said directly to you, right now, that his word is a foundational source that is reliable and will never change. It is so comforting to know that God and all of his promises will always remain consistent, no matter the valleys that life may put in your way.

Freedom & Deliverance

Write a response to today's devotion . Take a moment to reflect on what has stood out to you the most . What is God saying or speaking to you in today's devotional?

DAY

You are an overcomer! In Revelations 12:11 verse , The scripture tells us that we overcome by the blood of the lamb and the word of our testimony. Beloved , just as you are now in a season of grief, please know
that this season has an expiration date. As a believer in Christ, be assured that you have an expected end. No matter how bad things may seem right now, God
has a plan in it all. If you choose the abundant life that Christ has to offer you, I promise you that your end will be more glorious than your beginning. Know that as you endure the tranches of this time, God the Father is preparing your testimony and preparing you for victory. Yes, you will be victorious ! You will smile and laugh again. God promised you joy. Trust God that your new season will come.

Make this declaration today: My purpose is more significant than my present pain.

Testimony

Write a response to today's devotion . Take a moment to reflect on what has stood out to you the most . What is God saying or speaking to you in today's devotional?

____

____

____

____

____

____

____

____

____

____

____

____

____

DAY

The end is near and your healing is in sight. In this very moment, your healing is contingent upon hearing and receiving Holy Spirit inspired instructions. At the peak of my grief, I went to college away from home, friends, and all that was familiar to start a new life. The change was necessary. Although scary and confusing at the time, God had a unique plan in store for me. Now looking back, I understand that His plan for my life would not have benefited me if I did not receive the baptism of the Holy Spirit.

Getting to know the Holy Spirit during this time of grief is your secret weapon to achieve total and complete victory over grief. In the book of John Jesus says," But when He, the Spirit of truth, comes, He will guide you into all the truth. He will not speak alone; He will speak only what He hears, and He will tell you what is yet to come." The Holy Spirit has a way of directing you to the right place at the right time. Early in my grief process, the HolySpirit met me in a prayer service at a church I joined in my college town of Pine Bluff Arkansas. After-service, I packed my belongings and headed to the car. My Apostle Veronica stopped me and said she felt the Holy Spirit instructed her to pray for me.

I anxiously closed my eyes, and she started warring in prayer on my behalf, against the Spirit of grief that was severely attacking my mind, health, and overall quality of life. After prayer, I felt the demonic Spirit of mental oppression leave me immediately. She then instructed me to read the whole armor of God scripture for the next 30 days and to declare it over my life. Although, I didn't understand the fullness of Apostolic prophetic instructions. For some reason, I knew that I needed to follow these instructions to get to the other side of grief. I was obedient, and I experienced the miraculous. In that very experience, I learned that following the instructions of the Holy Spirit will always yield an abundant return in your life.

Holy Spirit

Write a response to today's devotion . Take a moment to reflect on what has stood out to you the most . What is God saying or speaking to you in today's devotional?

21 Scriptures of Healing and Deliverance

The next few pages are 21 bible scriptures on healing and deliverance. I ask that you read each scripture and declare it over your life and write a response to each scripture for the next 21 days, after doing this you will notice a considerable change and see the hand of God moving in your life.

Matthew 10:8 "Heal the sick, raise the dead, cleanse those who have leprosy, drive out demons. Freely you have received; freely give."

Psalm 30:2 "LORD my God, I called to you for help, and you healed me."

Mark 5:34 "He said to her, 'Daughter, your faith has healed you. Go in peace and be freed from your suffering.'"

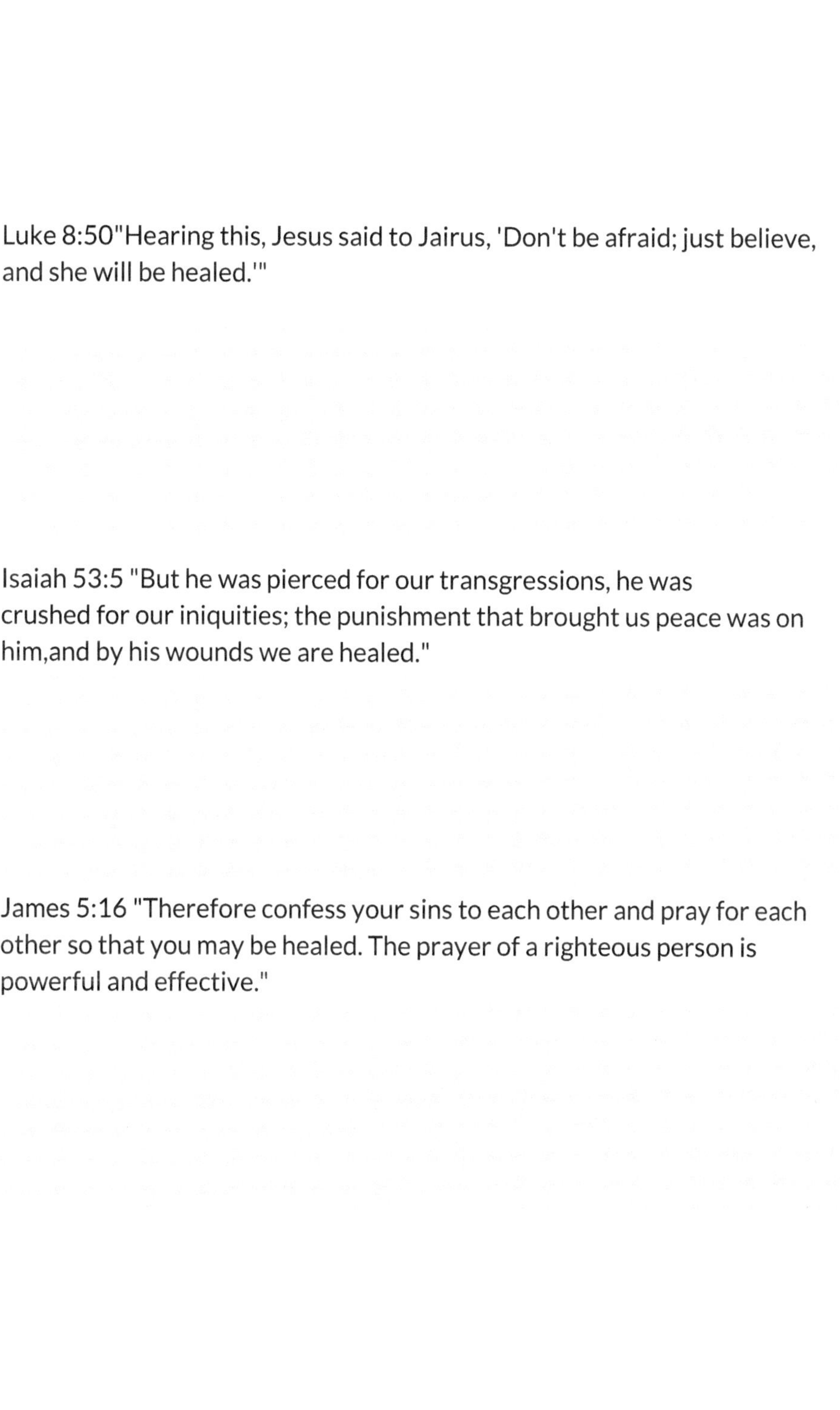

Luke 8:50"Hearing this, Jesus said to Jairus, 'Don't be afraid; just believe, and she will be healed.'"

Isaiah 53:5 "But he was pierced for our transgressions, he was crushed for our iniquities; the punishment that brought us peace was on him,and by his wounds we are healed."

James 5:16 "Therefore confess your sins to each other and pray for each other so that you may be healed. The prayer of a righteous person is powerful and effective."

Mark 10:52 "'Go,' said Jesus, 'your faith has healed you.'
Immediately he received his sight and followed Jesus along the road."

Psalm 147:3 "He heals the brokenhearted and binds up their
wounds."

Proverbs 17:22 "A cheerful heart is good medicine, but a crushed
spirit dries up the bones."

Revelation 21:4 "He will wipe every tear from their eyes. There will
be no more death' or mourning or crying or pain, for the old order of things
has passed away."

1 Peter 2:24 "'He himself bore our sins' in his body on the cross,
so that we might die to sins and live for righteousness; 'by his wounds you
have been healed.'"

Luke 10:9 "Heal the sick who are there and tell them, 'The
kingdom of God has come near to you.'"

James 5:14 "Is anyone among you sick? Let them call the elders
of the church to pray over them and anoint them with oil in the name of the
Lord."

. Psalm 107:20 "He sent out his word and healed them; he rescued
them from the grave."

Exodus 23:25 "Worship the LORD your God, and his blessing will be
on your food and water. I will take away sickness from among you."

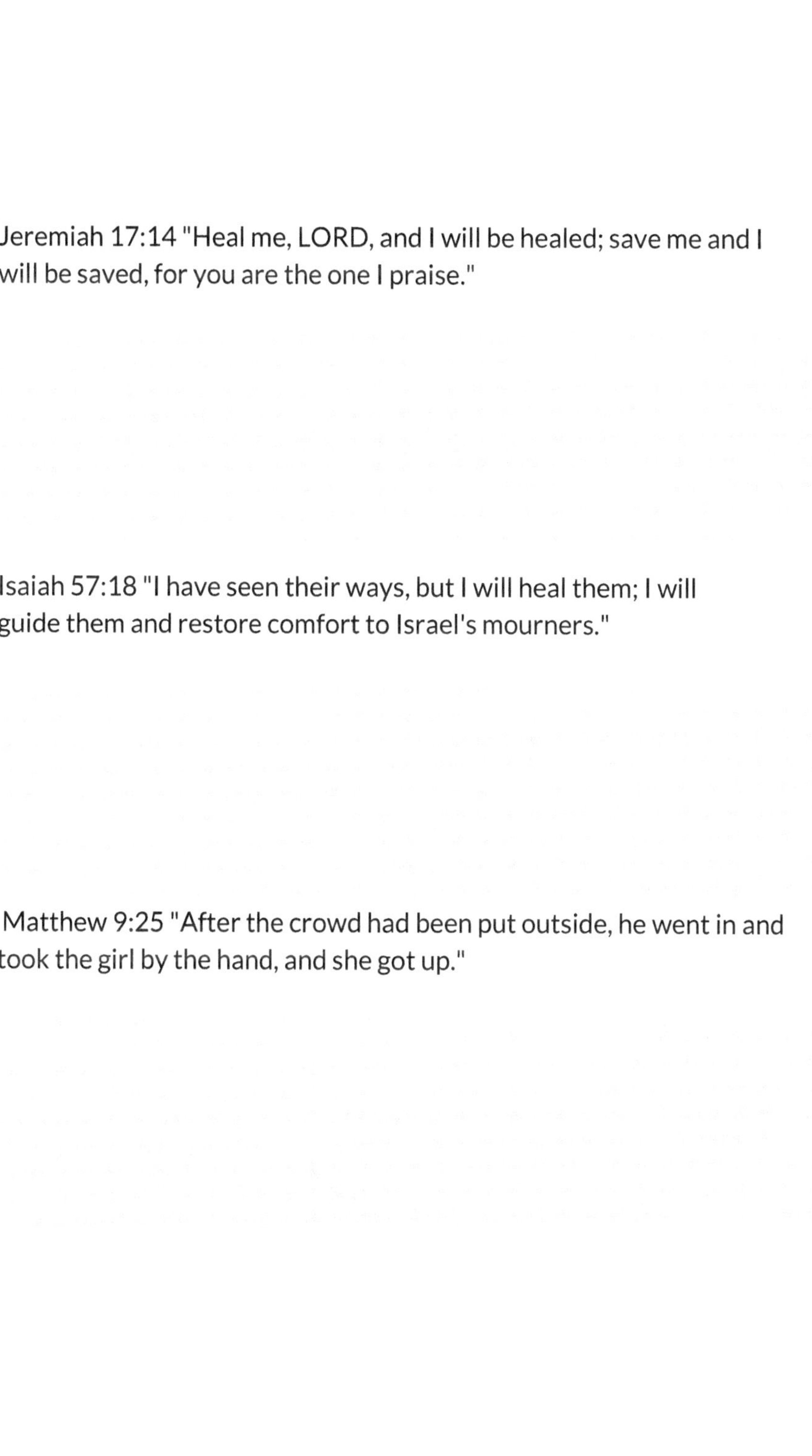

Jeremiah 17:14 "Heal me, LORD, and I will be healed; save me and I will be saved, for you are the one I praise."

Isaiah 57:18 "I have seen their ways, but I will heal them; I will guide them and restore comfort to Israel's mourners."

Matthew 9:25 "After the crowd had been put outside, he went in and took the girl by the hand, and she got up."

Acts 9:40 "Peter sent them all out of the room; then he got down on his knees and prayed. Turning toward the dead woman, he said,"Tabitha, get up." She opened her eyes, and seeing Peter she sat up."

Isaiah 19:22"The LORD will strike Egypt with a plague; he will strike them and heal them. They will turn to the LORD, and he will respond to their pleas and heal them."

Hosea 14:4 "I will heal their waywardness and love them freely, for my anger has turned away from them."

About The Author

Precious Jewel Taylor is a Minister of the Gospel of Jesus Christ. She is a first -year law student at Santa Barbara & Ventura Colleges of Law in Southern California. In her spare time, she enjoys spending time with family and friends and traveling the world. Precious hopes to one day use her Law degree in the area of Transactional Law while also working to serve underprivileged populations
in criminal Pro Bono cases.